IMAGES
of England

AROUND
STANLEY

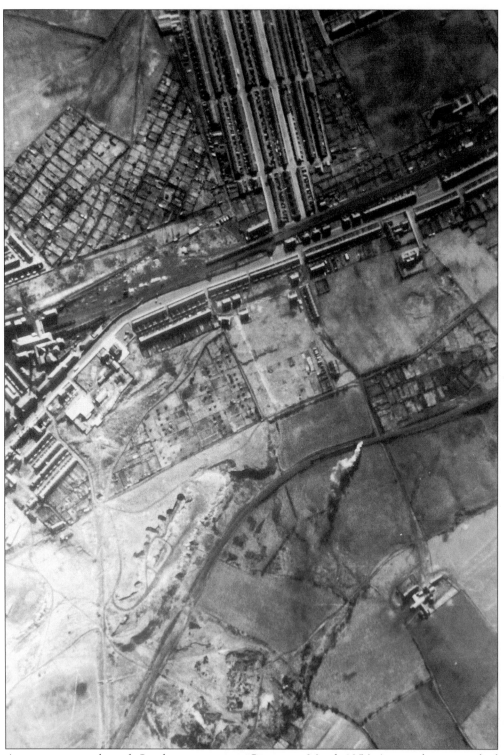

A train steaming through Stanley on its way to Consett in March 1956. An aerial view supplied by the Ministry of Defence (Crown Copyright).

2

IMAGES
of England

AROUND
STANLEY

Compiled by
Jack Hair and Alan Harrison

TEMPUS

First published 1997
Copyright © Jack Hair and Alan Harrison, 1997
Reprinted, 1998

Tempus Publishing Limited
The Mill, Brimscombe Port,
Stroud, Gloucestershire, GL5 2QG

ISBN 0 7524 0794 5

Typesetting and origination by
Tempus Publishing Limited
Printed in Great Britain by
Midway Clark Printing, Wiltshire

The centre of Stanley taken by the RAF in March 1956. An aerial view supplied by the Ministry of Defence (Crown Copyright).

Contents

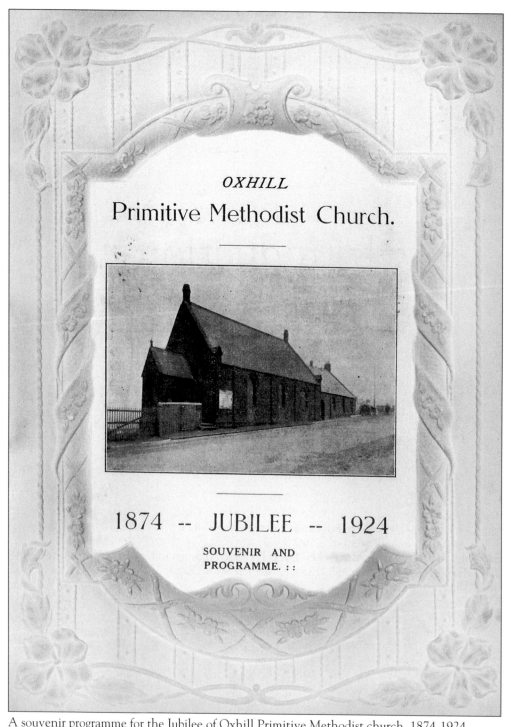

A souvenir programme for the Jubilee of Oxhill Primitive Methodist church, 1874-1924.

Introduction

On Stanley On.
(From the crest of Stanley Urban District Council,
later adopted by Stanley Comprehensive School.)

Visitors to Stanley today would not believe it was ever anything but a rural area surrounded by extremely beautiful countryside. Long gone are the many coal mines, waggonways, railways and pit heaps, which for over 150 years, were a living scar on the landscape.

The only reminders of that era are old photographs, the world famous Beamish Open Air Museum, Causey Arch and Tanfield Railway. Some early back-to-back housing still exists but even this is fast disappearing, being replaced by modern housing estates.

The known ancient history of the area goes back to AD 120-240 when there was a Roman Camp surrounded by a ditch (vallum) and turf walls. This camp was situated in the area behind what is now the Stanley Northern Bus Depot. Roman soldiers were stationed there to protect their cattle and sheep from marauding Scots. The soldiers lived in rough stone huts. In 1730, coins, swords, spears and pottery were discovered on this site by Sir Nicholas Tempest.

There was a Roman Road from South Shields into Stanley coming from Lawe Hill at Shields via White Mare Pool along to Wreken Dyke. It crossed through to Kibblesworth and Hedley to Causeway (Causey) and Stanley. It was a raised or secondary road laid directly on to ground level. The line the road took from Stanley is uncertain but in 1897, at the time of building Jubilee Terrace, New Kyo, excavations unearthed what is believed to be a section of this road going on to Lanchester.

At the time of William the Conqueror, Tanfield was listed as a Manor. The monks of Chester-le-Street had a church here around AD 900. They built a stone edifice around 1060 which was used for weekly service.

The first mention of the Lords of the Manor begins in the thirteenth century when Philip de la Leigh granted land between Shyleburn and Smaleburn named Stanleigh. Between 1233 and 1244, the land passed to the Almoner of St Cuthberts who in turn granted the lands to William de Kilkenny. His descendents became Lords of Stanley until the death of Richard de Kilkenny in 1394. The estate passed by marriage to John Danyell and then again by marriage to the widow of John de la Birtley. His son gave or exchanged the land to Sir Ralph Lumley. A tenant of the Lumley's, Robert Hall lived in Stanley Hall from 1470 until 1530 after which the land passed by charter to the Tempests who held the estate until 1733. A daughter of the Tempests married Lord Widdrington who passed it on by marriage to Peregrine Edward Towneley in the middle of the eighteenth century. This family owned 1,400 acres of land in Stanley and the district.

The coal owners were next to take over the land and very soon the area was criss-crossed with waggonways and pit heaps. Each coal mine was surrounded by housing for the miners and their families. Public houses began to be built, as well as churches, shops and schools. The major coal owners were; Burns & Clarke, Bowes and Partners, Morrison, Bell, Hunter & Hedley, Joicey and others.

At first the coals were drawn by pack mules but they were soon replaced with waggonways powered by steam driven standing engines. This was followed by the railways. Miners were brought in from all over Britain and beyond. For over 150 years these men and their descendants gave their all in the quest for coal, with many of them giving their lives.

By 1983 every single local coal mine had closed and miners needed to be retrained quickly. They proved very adaptable in new industries. Today, many of the younger generation know nothing of those days when coal was 'King'.

This book is not intended to be a history of Stanley, it is more a reflection of life in this area, before, during and since the coal industry. Most miners were proud of their job and totally loyal to their fellow miners. There was great comradeship in the hard task of drawing the coals out of the earth, nevertheless, many miners when they retired were thankful not to have to go down into the bowels of the earth ever again.

Acknowledgements

The authors would like to thank all those who have allowed us to use their photographs, including: Stanley Library, Beamish Museum, Derwentside Council, Jack Uren, George Nairn Michael Bailey, Michael Dodds, Ron Hindhaugh, Rita Brady, Chris Armstrong, Derek Hall, the late Wm Brown, E. Yard, The Ministry of Defence.

The authors have taken every care to check the facts for this book which are as accurate as the records available and that of people's own memories.

One
Around Stanley

Aerial view of Stanley, c. 1951. This photograph was taken from St Andrew's tower in the direction of Front Street.

Matt Armstrong's shop sign shows the Auctioneer and Emigration Office in Station Road. He also had a post office here from 1902 to 1935. He took over as postmaster from Andrew Mallams. The first post office in Stanley was in a shop adjacent to the Stanley Inn from 1871.

The Theatre Royal opened in 1903 with a seating capacity of 1,400. The total cost of the building and equipment was £15,000. On the frontage was a confectioners shop kept by Matt Ovington. The building was destroyed by fire in March 1930.

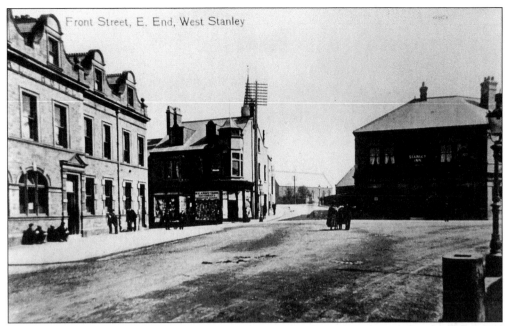

Lower Front Street, c. 1906. On the left is the Royal Hotel. In the centre is the post office and Emigration Office of Matt Armstrong. Just showing is the steeple of the Presbyterian church with St Andrew's church and the end of the National School. On the right is the Stanley Inn.

The Queen's Hotel, the large building on the left, opened in 1898 and was demolished in 1971. The advertising hoarding was the site later to be the Barclays Bank which opened in 1915.

11

Front Street, *c.* 1900. This snow scene is from an area well known for its severe winters. Many of the buildings shown were miners' houses later converted into shops.

Clifford Road, *c.* 1963. This road was originally only a tree lined path from Stanley to South Stanley and was named after Lord Clifford. He married Mable Ann Towneley in 1898 whose family were major landowners in Stanley.

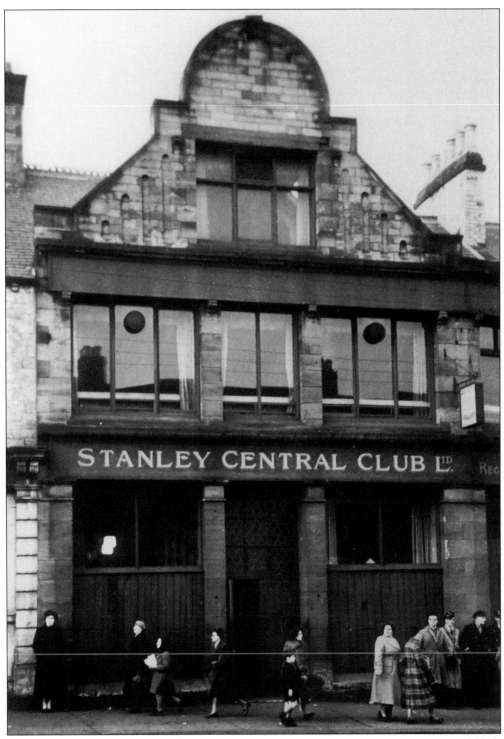

Stanley Central Club first began in Lower Front Street next to Pattison's newsagents in 1928. It then moved to the top of Blooms Avenue in 1938 before moving to this site on Front Street in premises once belonging to Trotters Dancing Academy.

Old Wesleyan chapel, *c.* 1895. In 1870 some members of Kip Hill Wesleyan chapel opened a meeting hall behind the Imperial Hotel. Other meeting places later were Joicey's Reading Rooms, the Co-op hall and rooms above stables behind the Commercial Hotel. They erected a tin chapel on the Council Offices site in 1880 and the church shown in the photograph in 1891.

New Wesleyan church, *c.* 1900. In 1898 work began on a larger church to accommodate 850 people. The old church was partly demolished and incorporated into the new building which was designed on the lines of Manchester Central Methodist church. The builder was A. Routledge and cost £4,500. It opened in May 1899 and was demolished in 1983.

The Old Civic Restaurant was at the lower end of Forster Street at the end of Peel Street. Meals could be eaten in either the restaurant or carried home. After it closed it became the Old Comrades Club which was known locally as the 'Ponderosa'. It closed around 1970.

The New Civic Restaurant, c. 1950. Councillor Mrs E. Brass opened the restaurant on 5 May 1949. The prefabricated building was in Scott Street and held 200 people. The manageress was Mrs M. Hunter. Unfortunately the restaurant closed after only eighteen months and was taken over by council surveyors and the housing department.

The Roller Skating Rink, *c.* 1907. Mr Murray of Consett purchased the land to build a public house but was refused planning permission. He sold the land to Mr Crawford who erected the roller skating rink which was open until around 1910 when it closed due to lack of support.

The Northern Bus Depot. The old skating rink was purchased by the newly formed bus company in 1914. Offices were added and the first services from the Stanley Depot began in May 1914 with six Daimler double-decker buses. The building was extended in 1922 and 1934, with major alterations in 1963.

High Street, c. 1925. In this view are the Pavilion Cinema, St Andrew's Institute and the National School. The Pavilion opened in April 1923 seating over 1,000 people. It had one of the first cinema organs installed in the north east which was dismantled and removed in January 1955 to make way for a bigger screen. The cinema closed in June 1966 and the final film was *Godzilla v The Thing*. The building later became a Bingo Hall and is now a motor parts shop with an Italian restaurant upstairs. The foundation stone for the church institute was laid on 12 June 1893 and it was opened on 9 July 1894. The Police Courts were held here until 1928. The church building, costing £1,600, had a billiard and news room, a good library and a hall seating 250 people. The National School, later West Stanley Infants School was built in 1867 for 308 children. It was enlarged in 1902 for 420 children. A temporary tin school was erected in 1912 for junior girls. The school was demolished in the early 1970s for the major redevelopment of the town.

Co-operative greengrocers and staff, *c.* 1910. West Stanley Co-operative was formed in 1876. The archway next to the shop was the entrance to the loading bay. The cobbled stone floor still exists.

Mr Caine the manager of the greengrocers with his staff in the backshop. This storage area is now the greengrocers shop of Mr John Hull.

West Stanley Co-op Society, No. 3 Jubilee Terrace, New Kyo, which opened for trading on 19 September 1925.

There was also a branch of West Stanley Co-op society in Shield Row. The opening ceremony was performed by Mr John Carr on Saturday 14 March 1925. The building is now a private house.

Moscardini's ice cream shop, 5 September 1951. Included in the photograph are Mrs Moscardini, Teresa Brixton, Joyce Bromley, Lily Haste and Olga Hodder. After the reduction of traffic from Front Street, the cafe eventually closed. It has since been Sam's Bar and is now an opticians.

Syd Wears, master butcher. Syd was born at Beamish in 1900 and moved with his family into the Stanley Inn in February 1909. He was fascinated with the butchery trade and often truanted school to help Henderson the butcher. As a boy he could skin a sheep as good as any man. He was apprenticed to Joe Dunn and opened his own shop in 1922.

Post office staff, c. 1950. On the right of the picture is Mr Cecil 'Tosh' Larmour who joined the post office after the Second World War. In the war he won the Military Medal for bravery in North Africa. Included in the photograph are Colin Bell, Betty Smith and Billy Lawson.

Post office staff. Back row, left to right: Colin Bell, Tom College, Fred Allaker, Betty Bates, Mabel Wilson, Len Clarke. Front row: Mrs Oakes, Charlie Mynott, Betty Stevens. The Clifford Road post office closed on 19 October 1991 and re-opened in Presto food store two days later.

The Prince of Wales visited Stanley on 29 January 1929 and again on 6 December 1934. On his second visit he laid the foundation stone for the Stanley Social Services building. Note the police on Stella Bridge.

Pavilion Temperance Bar, c. 1946. Rita McGarvey is outside the bar who, along with Ruby Beverley, assisted Pauline Vincenti in the ice cream parlour. The shop was opposite St Andrew's Institute. The Vincentis also owned a fish shop and off licence shop in the same block as the one shown.

Biagioni's confectioners, on Station Road just below the Market Hall. The shop also had a billiards and snooker table.

Stanley fire brigade, 1902. The brigade was formed in the late 1800s with volunteer members. The horse and cart belonged to a local trader and often the hardest job was catching the horse! Included in the photograph are: J. Parker, J. Scott, ? Smith, ? Twaites, ? Dunwoodie, ? Brown, Capt. T. Hazon, J. Hogarth, and driver M. Coxon.

Stanley Fire brigade, 1914. Though still part time, this brigade was formed from Council and Louisa Pit workers. The equipment was loaned from Louisa Colliery. In the event of large fires, Tyneside fire brigades were sent for.

The first full time fire brigade in Stanley wearing their new uniforms in 1939. They were based in the council yard. Back row, left to right: J. Peart, ? Sullivan, H. Harrison, S. Lurch, L. Carr. Middle row: B. Gracey, -?-, G. Peart snr, W. Watson, J. Storey, J. Jardine. Front row: ? Hetherington, ? Richardson.

Stanley Library, Anthony Street, 1963. This building was to the rear of Lloyds Bank. The library was opened on 29 April 1930 and before that the building had been Burdon's fish shop. In 1964 the library moved to new premises in High Street.

A view from the Pavilion, *c.* 1963. Most of these buildings were demolished in the redevelopment of the centre of Stanley. This area was replaced with a by-pass and roundabout.

The High Street showing the Salvation Army Citadel, the Law Courts and Police Station. Redevelopment seriously affected this area of Stanley.

The Victoria Cinema opened in March 1935 on the site of the former Victoria Theatre which had opened in June 1893. Bricks from the burned out Theatre Royal were cleaned and used on the inner walls of the new cinema.

Front Street with Dodgeson's newsagent in the foreground, with Doggart's drapery shop and the Classic (formerly Essoldo). The old Victoria Cinema became the Essoldo in 1948 and was a cinema until the mid 1970s. Beneath the old cinema was the Vic Billiard Hall which closed in 1968 and was converted for bingo.

Stewarts tailors, Front Street, *c.* 1920. The poster in the window is advertising a game at West Stanley AFC.

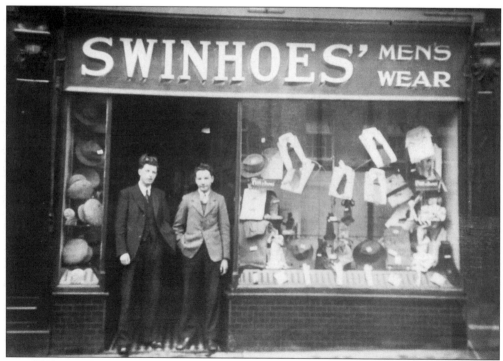

Swinhoes' gents outfitters was situated on Front Street opposite the Council Offices before the Second World War. John Wilson, left, returned after the war and eventually took over the shop.

Kingston's Umbrella Hospital, c. 1910. This shop was on Station Road below the Hibernian Hall. It was a gents hairdressers and during quiet periods the apprentices would repair umbrellas and make walking sticks.

Henderson's butchers was a family business which traded in Station Road for over fifty years from the turn of the century. They were noted for quality meat products mostly prepared on the premises.

A view looking up Stanley Street from the top of the Essoldo Cinema in October 1962.

Blackett's boot shop was at the junction of Front Street and Clifford Road. Blackett also had shops at Annfield Plain and Craghead Pit Yard. After he retired his wife opened a pie shop in the Front Street premises.

T. Scanlan's shop, *c.* 1930. This gents outfitters was at the lower end of Front Street. Zeta Welch, shown here, was the employee of Mr Scanlan.

M. Pattison's newsagents, *c.* 1920. This was his original shop which he took over from Thomas Ramshaw before moving along to the corner shop vacated by Wm Aynsley the grocer. Pattison retired in 1945 and the newsagents was taken over by Matt Dodgeson. The shop is now owned by Hemmings and Darwood.

J.R. Watson's family business first traded on Front Street as saddlers, hardware and cycle suppliers in the early 1900s. They later moved to Beamish Street where they also had a garage.

Jenny Moorcroft, left, and friend on Stanley Front Street with Swinburn's and Hunter's tea stores in view. Milk cart deliveries such as this continued until the 1940s.

Brough's grocers staff, c. 1903. The Stanley branch opened in 1902 in a block of four houses in Ramsey Street and the manager was Mr E. Fidell. The firm moved into Havanah House on Front Street in 1906. After a fire in 1914, new premises were erected.

At the front of the Council Offices is the memorial to the men and boys of the Burns Pit Disaster. The memorial was paid for by local workingmen's clubs. After many years it was moved to the entrance of Stanley Cemetery.

Empire Club, 1950. The club was originally formed in a building to the rear of the present premises. That old building, which had previously been a Methodist chapel and a billiards room, was destroyed by fire in 1915. The Empire was one of the first workingmen's clubs in the district and was affiliated to the Club Union in 1908.

Aerial view, *c.* 1960. In view is the junction of Church Bank and the High Street. The Presbyterian church is prominent with part of St Andrew's at the top of the picture. At the junction with High Street is the Stanley Inn known locally as Paddy Rocks and adjacent is the Tin School and the Church Institute.

Magistrates and councillors at the opening of the new Law Courts adjacent to Stanley Police Station in 1928. Prior to this, all local court cases were held in St Andrew's Institute.

Forster the brewer opened the Stanley Inn around 1860 as a double-fronted building. In the 1870s the post office was built on the east end of the building. The inn was rebuilt in 1898/99 and was finally demolished to make way for town redevelopment.

Tommy Muncaster's barber shop, *c*. 1930. This shop in Beamish Street was originally Jimmy Muncaster's radio shop. It was later converted into Tommy's hairdressers, confectioners and tobacconists. Included in the photograph are, George Harris, Tommy Muncaster and Ted Muncaster. Ted took over from Tommy and ran the shop until his death in 1966.

These houses at Joicey Terrace were built for miners between Stanley and Oxhill. One of the families who lived here was the Rodhams who later emigrated to America. One of their descendents is Hillary Clinton, the wife of President Clinton. The houses are now demolished with only one remaining.

Louisa Terrace, c. 1960. This terrace of miners' houses was first built in 1867. However, they were too small for families and were demolished and rebuilt in 1894 at the same time as Evelyn Terrace.

Councillor Ralph Powton removes the first turf at the Kings Head field to signify the start of the building of Stanley Baths in April 1963. The estimated cost was £200,000 and the baths were due for completion in March 1965. The opening was delayed and they were finally opened on Saturday 21 August 1965.

Shields Row Bank, c. 1910. On the left is Gordon Terrace leading up to South Thorn. On the right is Railway Terrace, which were Beamish Mary miners' homes, and North Thorn.

An aerial view of East Stanley, *c.* 1960. The first school in the area was erected in 1891 to hold approximately 300 pupils. There were extensions in 1896 and again in 1904. The school was demolished in the 1980s and painstakingly reconstructed at Beamish Museum. The headteacher's house is now a private dwelling.

East Street with the former ambulance station, left, and the Women's Institute, centre. The W.I. building was originally St Cuthbert's mission hall to St Andrew's. It was licensed for Divine Worship in 1896 but probably did not open until around 1900. It was a church and a hall and regular dances were held there. The church closed during the Second World War.

The Board Inn and fountain, *c.* 1950. The inn is probably the oldest licensed house in Stanley and was once known as 'Peacocks' after the family who ran it for many years. The fountain was erected in 1906 by the Eden family as a gift to the Urban District of Stanley. The water was shut off in May 1922 and the fountain was dismantled on 9 May 1954.

The Stanley Hotel at the top of Front Street was built in 1870 and Mr Charlton was the first landlord. Adjacent to the hotel was Hardy's furniture store opened in 1909 by Henry Cohan a Lithuanian. This was his first shop and he eventually owned seventy establishments from Scotland to Chatham.

St Joseph's church. The first Roman Catholic priest in Stanley was Father Matthews who travelled from Sacriston to say mass in the Board Inn. A school chapel opened in 1873. By 1893, Father Thompson had completed the presbytary. He also built St Joseph's church which cost £6,000 and opened in June 1902. Father Thompson was succeeded by Father (Canon) Dix.

A centenary procession of Thanksgiving from St Joseph's took place on 27 September 1972 when over 100 priests attended. The chief celebrant was Lord Bishop Cunningham who was joined by Father O'Brien, Revd Taylor, Revd Smith, Revd Brydon, Revd Warren and Lord Bishop Hagon. Children from St Joseph's and Towneley made up the offertory procession. They were, M. Lister, B. Spinks, M. Dawson and A. McConville.

St Joseph's School was erected by Father Matthews in January 1873. By 1890 it had fallen into great disrepair but was restored by Father Thompson. In 1908 Father Dix extended the school.

St Andrew's church. Revd Crennell built the new parish church in 1876 on land gifted by Squire Eden of Beamish and it was opened in December of that year. The vicarage was built in 1879 costing £1,630. The Celtic Cross was erected in 1923 in memory of the men of the parish. The church was extended in 1931.

General Booth visiting the barracks in Stanley High Street in 1911. Booth once described his mission in life to his son as that of a 'Salvation Army', and the name stuck. While at Stanley he stayed with Dr W. Benson. He spoke to a mass audience at the Theatre Royal in Station Road. He died the next year aged 83.

The Salvation Army Sunbeams outside the High Street Citadel, c. 1949. Included are, Captain and Mrs Jenks, June Kirk, Irene Hunter, Audrey Hall, June Errington, Christine Wright, Lestrine Almond and Elizabeth Raynor.

St Andrew's church extension, Friday 27 June 1930. The stone laying ceremony was performed by Rt Hon. Arthur Joicey with the afternoon service conducted by the Bishop of Durham. The extension cost £9,000 and included the installation of the bells. There were donations of £1,000 each from Lord Joicey and Mrs Charlton of Wylam. The extension was consecrated on 14 January 1931.

The procession for the opening of St Stephen's church on 26 June 1954 which included the clergy and choir headed by the Bishop of Durham, Revd A.M. Ramsey. The church doors were opened by the Bishop and Mrs S. Atkins, the daughter of George Watson who bequeathed £15,000 towards the total cost of £18,000.

View Lane church. Stanley Primitive Methodists began in the kitchens of Jane Luke and Betty Gilcrest at Shields Row in 1823. In 1853 they moved into two converted cottages behind No. 5 North Thorn. The View Lane church opened in 1864. The first Manse was built in 1869 and the church was extended in 1873. The View Lane Manse was built in 1909 and the Lecture Hall opened in 1932 costing £1,512.

Revd Purdy of South Stanley Methodists with some of the young members on the steps of their church. When it was first built in 1959, the church, adjacent to Cleveland Terrace, was very successful. However, support dropped off and the church was demolished in 1969.

The Garden House Club, c. 1930. The club was first formed in allotment gardens near Spen Street around 1900, moving into No. 39 Spen Street in January 1913. They then transferred to Tyne Road in the early 1920s where these officials are shown.

The Hibernian Club committee, 1945. They include: B. Connelly, J. Martin, T. Burg, F. Duffy, J. Hughes, T. Ryan, J. McGee, J. Davis, G. O'Neil, B. Whitney, ? Doran, Mr Martin, P. Lavin, T. McGee, ? Carney. The Irish League first met in the Royal Hotel around 1900. They opened their first club above Castles jewellery shop (now Margaret's Cafe) in 1902/03. They then built the Station Road club in 1907 which was opened the following year.

Venture bus at Oxhill, c. 1955. This company was one of the oldest independent bus companies in the north east beginning just after the First World War. By 1960 they were operating eighty-five buses. They introduced one man operation by 1959, eight years before Northern who bought the Venture company in 1970.

New Causey Road. Plans for this road from Kip Hill to Sunnyside were drawn up in 1930. These plans were abandoned and an alternative road of 1.75 miles was adopted costing £116,532. In all 1,106 unemployed men were used on its construction as a condition of their unemployment benefit. The road was opened by Alderman J. Jeffrey on 23 June 1934.

A view from the roof of the Northern Garage, *c.* 1950. It shows Slaideburn Road, the Kings Head and the Northern Employees' Club. Also in view are St Andrew's church and the steeple of the Presbyterian church (United Reform).

The Northern bus service from Newcastle to Stanley at Bewick Street. The bus shown is CN 1596, an ex-RAF tender 14-seater purchased in 1922. It was based at the Stanley Depot.

Stanley Council chambers, 1950. W. Jolley is in the chair. Also at the meeting are Mrs I. Jolley, Norman Seymour, Mrs Charlton, Dr Ludkin, J.J. Shipston and Mr Niven. The Council first held its meetings in the National School before hiring a room in the bank at Chaytor's buildings. They then moved to Forster's undertakers' back rooms, which is now in the region of Woolworths, before the Front Street Council Offices were built.

Councillors in Avon Road inspect one of the first elderly persons' bungalows built by the council in 1932. The Councillors and staff include: Messrs Sasbry, Tucker, Pearson, Burleigh, Pattison, L. Kelly, Mrs I. Jolley, B. Kelly, Vince, Burridge, Hudspith and Hamilton. Mrs Jolley was the first lady councillor to be elected to Stanley Council.

Prefabs Coronation Party, 1952. This was held in the scout hut on the Kings Head field to celebrate the coronation of HRH Queen Elizabeth II. Some of those included are, Margaret, Susan and Beaulah Watson, Rose, Vivian and Dickie Richards, Mary and Pat Adams, Annie Bates, Betty Bennett, David Wilson, Theresa Finnegan and Arnold Armstrong. Among the women are, Mrs Watson, Mrs Bennett, Mrs Bates, Mrs Rodham and Mrs Wilson.

Stanley Board School was built during 1891 and 1892 and opened 17 August 1892. The first headteacher was Mr Robert Wilson Little. On that first day there were 93 pupils. By the end of the first week there were 200 pupils. The school was extended in 1898.

These cottages were built before 1851 near Sunny Terrace. They were for the miners of Oakey's and West Shield Row Colliery and were demolished in 1934 after the closure of the colliery in the same year.

Joicey Square. When they were built these houses were known as New Stanley. Anderson shelters, visible in the photograph, were built during the Second World War. The corrugated iron shelters were covered with grass turf, soil and sand. After the war, Len Simpson, then aged seven, was trapped when the materials covering one of the shelters cascaded down and buried him. He was rescued by a neighbour.

The Louisa Coke Works, where the Louisa Sports Centre now stands. Recently, when the slip road into the Netto food stores beside the Sports Centre was being built, narrow rail lines were uncovered. These lines formerly ran into the coke works.

Albert 'Jinks' Harrison of Towneley Street with his son Jimmy and dog Billie. While walking his dogs Billie and Tinker around the council ash tip on 13 November 1948, he came upon the murdered body of Sarah Ellen Watson. A local man was convictd for the killing and sentenced to twelve years imprisonment. Jinks' reward was to be fined for not having a dog licence!

'Sticky' Bainbridge originally traded in a shop adjoining the Smiths Arms at Old South Moor vacated by Micky Martin in 1892. He later moved into the South Moor shop. He had a cork leg and was the first man in South Moor to own a car.

Henry Street, one of several streets forming Gas House Square. The Gas Works are in the background, situated in the area now between the present day library and the Mormon church of Jesus Christ and Latter Day Saints.

This Church Lads Brigade was based at St Andrew's church during the First World War. They had an excellent rifle shooting competition record. Note the small cannon.

Board School pupils being instructed by Miss Robinson (Mrs Masterman) in the school yard in 1939. The group is learning to play the mouth organ.

Two
Collieries

Beamish Mary miners, 1898. The miners are just about to descend into the mine. One of them is Jack Wears. This colliery, opened in 1884, closed in April 1966 when 400 men were either transferred or made redundant.

'The Fortune Pit' by Jim Bradley. This is a copy of one of four watercolours painted by Jim. The Burnhope pits opened in 1844. Four men died in a shaft accident in 1893 when a rope broke. They were: G. Holt, A. Laycock, J. Hall and G. Shaw.

The Delight Pit, Dipton. This colliery was sunk in 1842 and a second shaft in 1853. In 1855 William Elliott, aged 11, fell down the shaft. There was great disruption at the colliery due to strikes in 1879.

Margaret Pit, Tanfield Lea. 3986

Tanfield Lea Margaret Pit. Joicey took over the Tanfield Lea collieries in 1842. The colliery welfare was formed in 1930 and pit head baths introduced in 1954. In 1961, the United States Air Force Band played the lodge banner into the Durham Miners Gala. This colliery closed in August 1962.

Tanfield Lea surface workers in front of the winding engine wheel. It is incredible that these wheels were capable of lifting great weights for years and years.

Tanfield Moor Colliery. This pit was sunk in 1768 for the Earl of Kerry. By 1810 the owner was William Pitt and there were four seams working. Before closure, in 1947, the colliery was owned by Lambton, Hetton and Joicey.

Oakey's heapstead fire, 1909. The fire virtually destroyed the winding gear and surface buildings. The pit opened in 1783 and closed in 1934.

Jackie's Pit was situated between East Stanley and No Place. Sinking began in 1863 and the shaft bottom reached by 1864. There are mentions of a chapel at Jackie's Pit. In 1930 Joicey sold the colliery to the Derwent Coal company who closed it in 1937.

'Burnhope Pit Yard' by Jim Bradley showing Office Row, Cross Row and Stone Row. The miners' houses could hardly have been closer to the pit head.

This ambulance team is at Hustledown Rescue Station. The miners' welfare fund was used to finance the ambulance which was a great improvement on the former horse-drawn, straw-laden, carts previously used to transport injured miners home or to hospital.

The Morrison Busty. The Morrison North and South pits were sunk in 1868. Shortly after this they built a double battery of beehive coking ovens. The pit was idle from 1876 to 1891. The South Pit closed in 1948. The Busty was sunk in 1923 and opened in 1927 with shafts east and west.

The main shaft of the Louisa Pit was sunk in 1863/4. The Shield Row shaft was sunk in 1883, drawing coals in 1884. The last coals were drawn from the Louisa on Saturday 20 January 1956. The colliery was sold to Stanley Urban District Council in 1966.

East Tanfield Colliery miners, c. 1900. This colliery opened in 1844. Pit head baths were installed in 1958 and the pit closed in 1964.

Wm Hedley jnr, right, observes the Wylam Dilly at Craghead in 1862. His father, William snr, sank the Craghead William Pit in 1839. When he died in 1843 he was succeeded by his sons, Thomas, William, George and Oswald, with William jnr the dominant partner.

Stanley Bankhead was situated at East Stanley and was part of the Stanhope & Tyne Railway, opened in 1834. The Stanley Level, $2\frac{1}{2}$ miles long, was worked by horses to the Bank Head. This was followed by a series of self acting inclines. The first being 1,276 yards long was Stanley Bank. The line was dismantled in 1952. The photograph is from the J.W. Armstrong Collection, courtesy of Tanfield Railway Society.

The pit sinkers in the 1890s. These were the first men to arrive at any colliery and were the first to be housed. The method of sinking was slow due to the lack of mechanisation.

The Craghead Colliery Band was formed in 1910. One of their finest achievements was to win the North of England championships in 1924. The colliery closed in 1968.

South Moor Band, c. 1960. The band was formed in 1892 but did little in competitions until they purchased a new complete set of instruments in 1903. After that they went from strength to strength. They are shown in South Moor Park just before the Durham Miners Gala.

South Tanfield Colliery Band was one of the first in the area. The colliery at Oxhill was sunk in 1837 with a second shaft in 1839. A third shaft was sunk in 1870. The colliery closed in 1914 and was demolished in 1921.

Miners Sunday, c. 1960. Union officials, miners and their families paraded through Stanley to Murray Park for Miners Sunday. There was a Service of Thanksgiving, prayers and hymn singing with all the church leaders taking part.

Rescue team, *c.* 1920. The Rescue Station was erected at Hustledown in 1912/13 by the South Moor Coal Co. The men are pictured at the rescue station in full equipment. One of their largest rescues in the 1920s was at the nearby Hedley Pit when it took almost two days to bring the 150 men to the surface.

Pit ponies and their drivers. The drivers are: left to right, T. Davidson, T. Massie, W. Brown, J. Walker. The ponies are: Raven, Roany, Stoker and Happy.

Burnhope Colliery Band and banner at the miners' hall, Burnhope. They are just about to set off for Durham City for the Gala.

Marley Hill Colliery opened in 1841 and closed on 3 March 1983. After the closure 733 miners found jobs at other pits, 33 were made redundant and 160 were kept on a temporary basis for salvage work. Most of the ponies were retired.

The Louisa, Morrison Old North Pit Disaster, 1947. At 11.45 pm on 22 August 1947, there was a serious explosion 450 feet underground and twenty-one men lost their lives. Nineteen died instantly while the other two died of their injuries. The official cause was that firedamp from the strata below the Hutton Seam created a mixture of firedamp and air on the East Face Line and the Straight East Gate. Shortly before midnight a Lucifer match was struck about the Loading Point on the Straight Line Gate. This ignited the mixture causing a mild explosion which developed additional force propagated by coal dust along the mechanical roadways. It was finally extinguished by stone dust at the south heading of the Main Drift. Rescue workers William Younger, Joseph Shanley and Harry Robinson were doing normal safety work within 200 yards. They toiled with total disregard for their own safety bringing out five men and were commended for their bravery. It was later believed that electrician T. Makepiece, should also have been commended for bravery. The miners were taken to the ambulance room at the North Pit. Dr Fox and Dr Josephs confirmed the deaths of the nineteen whose bodies were removed to the joiners' shops. Four blacksmiths, Ted Errington, J. Cook, W. Jobling and T. Robinson were due to do a job in the area of the explosion. As the replacement part was not there, they came out of the pit and returned to the Louisa knowing nothing of the explosion and tragedy until later. They were very lucky men. The survivors were; Clement Minto, William Johnson, J. Killgallon. The miners killed were: H. Talbot, A. Bailey, E. Westgarth, J. Estello, T. McKever, R. Birtle, W. Roe, F. Martin, T. Appleby, J. Rowland, G. Moore, W. Reed, T. Bell, T. Bell (second of this name), J. Hodgson, N. Fenwick, J. Chapman, C. Simpson, R. Brown, J. Grimley, W. Rutherford. (Photograph from *Stanley News*, 23 August 1947)

Three
Annfield Plain

This postcard includes views of St John's Methodist church, the Cenotaph in the park, Front Street, Catchgate Road Ends and the Morrison Colliery.

Front Street. On the right are Swinburne & Co's Queen Head Hotel, the level crossing and box, and in the distance St Johns's Methodist church. On the left is the gents' underground toilets.

Annfield Plain Secondary Modern School was opened in 1914 and was known locally as the 'Upper Standard'. The all girls school was upstairs and the boys school downstairs. The schools had separate headteachers.

St Aidan's church. In 1898 a small mission church was erected behind the Tin School. The foundation stone for St Aidan's was laid on 25 August 1928. The new church was built by J. Jackson & Sons and was opened by the Bishop of Durham in 1929 when the vicar was Revd T. Dick.

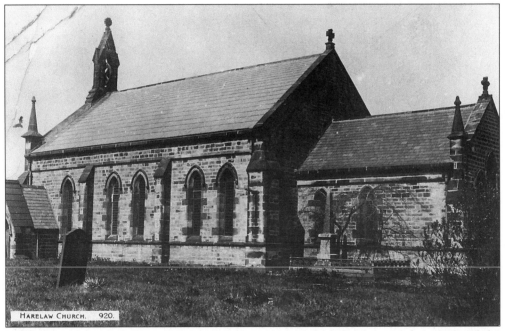

HARELAW CHURCH. 920.

St Thomas' church, Hare Law. The foundation stone was laid on 15 September 1840 and the church opened in July 1841. The belfry was blown down in a storm in 1853. Mission churches were built at Greencroft in 1929 and West Kyo in 1930. The vicarage was built in 1858 costing £1,150.

Pontop Pike Television Mast, 1954. The photograph shows the booster relay unit of the temporary station with a 300 foot mast. It sent out its first pictures on 1 May 1953. It was extended to 500 feet on 11 November 1955. A Pye TV set then sold at 67 guineas and a TV/Radio licence was £2.

CATHERINE TERRACE, NEW KYO.

Reece's shop, New Kyo. This former newsagents shop is now owned by Mr Clish. This street is one of the oldest in New Kyo.

An accident involving a bus and other vehicles under the bridge leading to Annfield Plain Railway Station. The station was opened in 1894 and closed to passenger traffic in 1955.

Central Methodist church. In March 1993 the church was destroyed when a 17-year-old girl set fire to the building. It was decided to rebuild the church and services were held at St Thomas'. In December 1993, an outdoor Thanksgiving Service was held and Mr Wright the minister spoke of it being a rebuilding of strength. The restored church opened again on 5 November 1994.

Annfield Plain, Gleemen, 1903. Some members of the local methodist church decided to form a separate male voice choir, which eventually became the 'Gleemen'. Practices were held in the home of accompanist Tom Turner. The first conductor was Chris Mordue.

The Willie Pit cottages, c. 1925. By 1925 the cottages were in great need of repair or demolition. Only the wooden supports prevented the houses from falling down of their own accord. The Willie Pit was sunk in 1866.

74

Doris and Nora Wilson, Mr and Mrs Gilmore and Mrs Cook at Greencroft Towers. This gateway was the eastern approach to Greencroft Hall supposedly built by Sir Thomas Clavering. He held the estate from 1794 to 1853. In 1840 it was called Greencroft Portal. The tower had a gothic arch flanked by two cottages, one on each side.

Due to subsidence the tower that stood in the gap had been in danger of collapse. Restoration costs were estimated at £3,940 so it was decided to demolish it and this took place in April 1955. The remaining arch collapsed while the workmen were away from the site and the families who occupied the cottages had to leave their houses by the windows.

Dipton St John's under snow in 1947 when heavy falls blocked all the surrounding roads. The parish of Dipton was formed in 1883 and early services were held in the Board School. Work began on St John's in 1885 and the church and graveyard were consecrated in July 1886, costing £3,400.

The snow around the Plough Inn was so deep that clearance was impossible and so the snow was just left to thaw.

Ringtons Tea Store in a snow drift, Hare Law, 1947. A cup of tea would have been useful in this weather! Ringtons has traded in the district for many years.

The Hobsons built a corn mill at Harperley in 1819. The mill was driven by water from Kyo Burn. The building was later converted into Tanfield Lea Workingmen's Club before they moved to their present site. It then became Harperley Hotel on a licence formerly held by the Rose Cottage Inn at West Kyo.

Durham Road looking towards the centre of the town. The Infant School was situated on the left near the bridge and was a corrugated tin structure built in 1897. It was finally dismantled in 1988.

Annfield Plain Road Ends. This is the end of Shield Row Lane which runs from Kip Hill to Annfield Plain and is one of the oldest roads in the district. The buildings to the right are the old National Assistance Offices.

A Northern Daimler bus, No. J4902-D24, on the Chester-le-Street to Consett route. It is pictured at Johnson's shop in West Road Annfield Plain. Note the solid wheels.

West Road with the Coach and Horses Inn on the right. The Coach and Horses was a 'Jerry', a public house with a beer licence only. The inn was demolished in November 1965 and a new pub built on the site. Further up the bank can be seen the headgear of the Willey Pit.

Annfield Pit Co-operative society was formed in 1870 on the site where the Democratic Club is now. This was the first shop opened on 17 May 1870. The first of the central premises were built

in 1873 with a new suite of shops added in 1925. The Co-op store was demolished in the mid 1970s and reconstructed in Beamish Museum.

Ash midden toilets like these in Gorecock Terrace were common to the area. The wooden toilet seat lifted to allow coal fire ashes to cover the waste. Old newspapers cut into squares were used as toilet paper. Council workers called weekly to empty the middens. It was a long, cold walk to toilets like these.

Romsome & Marles, a Government assisted bearings factory, opened on the Greencroft Industrial Estate in 1953 to offset the loss of jobs in the declining mining industry. Many miners were successfully retrained in new skills.

Four
Burnopfield

Busty Bank, *c*. 1880. To the right is the United Methodist Free church, built around 1869. The extension to the church plus the building of a Sunday School and caretaker's house began in 1906 and were completed for re-opening by Easter 1903.

Leazes School, 1894-1968. Tanfield School Board bought the land for this school from J.B. Eden for £879 in 1893. The builders, Mr A. Davis & J. Thomas quoted £2,325 11s 0d. The Board borrowed £3,500, to be paid back over 50 years. The school opened 8 January 1894.

Burnopfield School was built in 1933 as a Secondary Modern. The first headteacher was Mr Bell in 1937 followed by Mr Mackerell from 1933-54. The last headteacher at the secondary school was Mr J. Uren from 1954-68 after which it changed to a junior school.

Busty Bank is believed to have got its name from a coal seam which, exposed to the frost and rain, burst its bank from a drift mine with coals falling on to the road. The house, top right, is now the Burton House pub. All the other buildings survive.

Burnopfield Co-operative store. The hall adjacent to it was once the Grand Cinema and Billiards Hall. The Co-op opened in the 1860s with two departments – provisions and drapery. A butchers shop was added and later still a new hall and several cottages.

The road past the Sun Inn, *c.* 1890. There were several cottages leading up to the Sun Inn on the left. To the extreme right is a building known as the Black House. Also on the right was a bungalow used by Father Matthews for Roman Catholic services.

A view opposite the Travellers from Leazes toward Burnopfield in the 1920s. The Travellers is known locally as Jack Allan's. He played football for Newcastle United at the time of Hughie Gallacher. The Temperance Hall on the right was built in 1872 and is now St James' Hall.

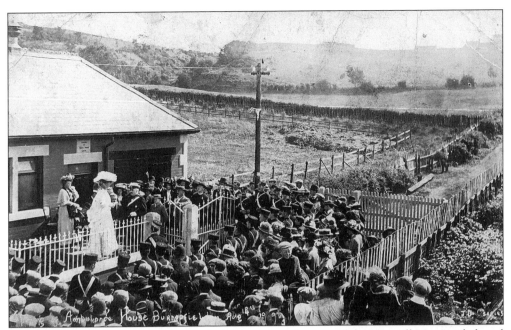

The ambulance station, *c.* 1909. This building was to the rear of the Haswell Memorial chapel and the opening service was carried out by Miss Watson, the daughter of Dr Watson of Burnopfield House. The ambulance station was later converted into a two storey building.

The Old Wesleyan chapel was built in 1775 by Sheep Hill stonemason William Bickerton. John Wesley preached there on his last four visits to the region. The old pulpit from which he preached and a pane of glass behind the pulpit dated 1780 were preserved and placed in New Haswell Memorial church in 1879.

The murdered doctor's bridge. The Co-op horse and cart with driver Mr J. Iley is shown at the bridge leading to Rowlands Gill. On 1 November 1855 Dr Stirling left to visit High Spen and was last seen at 1.00 pm in Smailes Lane. A local farmer heard a shot but Dr Stirling's body was not found until 6 November. He had been shot, his throat cut and his possessions stolen.

The fountain situated in the area known as Bryans Leap was erected by Miss A. Rippon in 1906. Sadly she died before it was completed. The memorial was accepted by H.C. Woods on behalf of the parks committee and by W. Bulmer JP on behalf of Tanfield U.D.C.

The caretakers of Gibside Hall outside the entrance. The estate had 4,000 acres and was built between 1603-20. In 1804 there were 324 paintings in the hall.

The village blacksmith, c. 1900. The blacksmith was very important to village life. Most of his work was shoeing horses but he would also have made and repaired farm implements and tools. The blacksmith is possibly Matt Hunter.

Syke Road from Hobson to Leazes was originally named Long Sykes Bank. Low Friarside Farm was once situated in the fields to the left and visible on the left is St James' church. To the right is Leazes School.

Pantomime at the Hobson, c. 1950. Members of the Hobson Methodist church taking part include: Mavis Yard, Sadie Beck, Jean Beck, Jenny Davidson, Anne Stephenson, Verna Parker, Joyce Powton and Alice Forster.

Five

Craghead

Craghead Colliery offices, *c.* 1910. There were several shafts over the years the first being the William Pit sunk by William Hedley snr in 1839. The colliery finally closed in 1968.

The old Co-op store. This old shop was the original Craghead Co-op built in the 1800s on the same site as the later Co-op. The butchers shop was on the corner with the manager's house next door. These shops were later enlarged but were demolished in 1981.

Edward Terrace was an important street in Craghead. On the left are; the school, Hedley Memorial Hall, the War Memorial, the fire station hut and the Punch Bowl public house. On the right are houses, local shops and the Co-op.

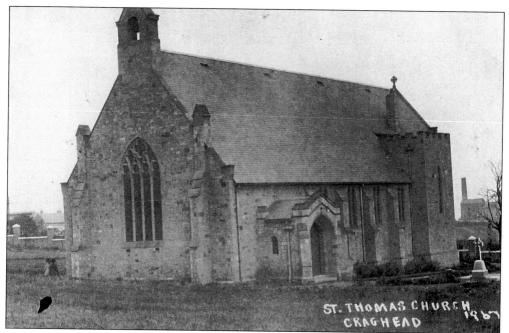

St Thomas' church. A licence was granted for a mission church in 1884. Early services were held in the Co-op reading rooms and the infant school in John Street. A tin mission church opened in 1900 on the site of the present vicarage. The burial ground opened in 1907. The new church costing £3,750 opened on 17 July 1911.

Shafto House, erected by the Hedleys, c. 1850. It was once the home of colliery viewer James Fairley. Dr Fox married one of Mr Fairley's daughters and lived in the adjacent Shafto Cottage.

A Northern bus and crew stand at the crossroads opposite Craghead Co-op. The bus is a Daimler Y type No. J2118-D28. It was fitted with a Dodson single deck body. The driver is G. Scott, the conductor H. Robinson and the inspector W. Armour.

At 11.15 am on Tuesday 25 September 1951, an RAF twin jet Meteor aeroplane piloted by Pilot officer F. Rogers crashed on South Moor Golf Course, 400 yards south west of the club house. The plane was buried 15 feet into the ground.

Craghead Show, c. 1960. This was a very successful show with a parade including decorated carts. There were also stalls, boxing and other sports.

John Mitchison and his family farmed Fawside Farm, Craghead. He is shown working his horses in the field adjacent to St Thomas' church. His brother farmed Flats Farm near Burnhope.

Bloomfontein School, 1951. Jimmy Larmour is sixth from the left in the back row.

A soup kitchen in Burnhope during the 1926 strike when there was great hardship. The Co-operative movement, churches and schools donated food and cooking equipment. Surprisingly, even some local coal owners gave assistance.

Six

Tanfield

Tanfield church. There has been a church in the village since around 900, built by monks from Chester-le-Street. A new church was built in about 1050. In 1724 a new church bell was purchased for £7. In 1736, Curate R. Wilson caused the church to collapse by mining for coal beneath the building! The church was rebuilt in 1750. The first peel of the new bells were heard in June 1891. In 1874 St Margaret's was greatly improved.

Tanfield Hall was first built as a manor house and was once the vicarage of Revd Jos. Simpson from 1790-1830. In 1788, when the Spearman family lived there, part of the roof fell in killing one child and injuring another. The gates were made by the village blacksmith in 1730 and were restored in 1958.

Tudor House stood behind the Peacock Inn on land known as 'The Square'. The red tiled building was a local landmark in the eighteenth century. It was later converted into flats but was vandalised in 1928 and fell into ruin. It was once a school and offices for the Workhouse. It was demolished in 1958.

Canon Archdale came to Tanfield in 1877 and served as a magistrate, councillor and Guardian of the Poor. He was also the DLI 5th Battalion chaplain for over 50 years. He is pictured with his wife and family on the pair's 50th wedding anniversary in April 1923. Canon Archdale served Tanfield church for 47 years until his death in June 1924.

A view of the village, *c.* 1900. For many years Tanfield was the commercial and religious centre for the surrounding area. There was a grammar school, a church school and a hospital. There was also a weekly market where landowners could hire workers. Tanfield was also the centre for local entertainment.

Causey Arch. Prior to 1726 there was a rail line from Causey to Dunston. The arch was built for Col. Liddle and the Hon. Charles Montague (the 'Grand Allies') to obtain a level passage for the coal wagons, bridging the Causey Burn with a span of 103 feet. The arch was built by mason Ralph Wood costing £12,000. He committed suicide following the collapse of an arch he had built.

A typical winter scene in Tanfield Lea, *c.* 1960. Epworth Methodist church and the Co-op are in the background.

Woodside Methodist church. On 26 January 1878 a Primitive Methodist chapel was opened at Low Winning costing £839. The foundation stone at Woodside was laid in 1912 and the new church opened in January 1913 costing £2,387. The Diamond Jubilee was held around 1929.

The steep hump in the road between Tanfield Lea School and Hunter's Garage was removed in two stages to allow the traffic to keep moving. Note Hunter's bus coming over the hill.

Tanfield Lea Co-operative. This branch of West Stanley Co-operative opened in 1923. There was some dispute with the nearby Tantobie Co-operative but this was soon resolved. The two Co-operatives were united in 1925.

This is the public telephone box during the Second World War. Because of the importance to Tanfield Lea it was camouflaged and protected against enemy bombers.

The Tanfield Lea Colliery Welfare held an annual sports day in the village school field. The children competed in sports events for small prizes and they were all provided with a picnic.

The village postman, *c.* 1900. Tanfield village had a postal collection service long before Stanley. The Hagar Directory of 1851 names the Tanfield postmaster as Robt. Todd Wakefield. The Whellans Directories of 1857 and 1865 name the postmaster as Martin Watson.

Epworth Methodist church, *c.* 1950. The choir was conducted by Mr Norman Williams. Epworth church opened 3 April 1874. The new Sunday School and caretaker's house were built in 1898/9. After closure it became a clothing factory and is now an old people's home.

Seven

The Burns Pit Disaster

In 1909 Stanley was a typical mining town with back to back houses built close to the pit. It was a cold, windy town of miners and their families, standing on ten seams of fine coking coal. The Burns & Clarke Colliery was sunk in 1832.

On Tuesday 16 February 1909 a muffled explosion rocked the town and 50 seconds later there was a second explosion with flames shooting into the sky. There could be no doubt that the Burns Pit had exploded. Panic followed and there was an instant movement of people towards the pit head, in no time at all there were thousands at the stricken colliery.

Gathering at the pit head. There was little organisation as Mr Hall the manager was away seeking another job. Mr Fairley, the manager of South Moor Collieries, arrived and started to organise the situation.

The pit head wheel had stopped and the electric fuses had blown, cutting off the underground air current. Mr Ralph Stephenson, the colliery engineer, was closest to the explosion and looked down the North Shaft where there was a red glow. As he stood back a ball of fire leapt into the sky then the smoke was sucked back down into the pit.

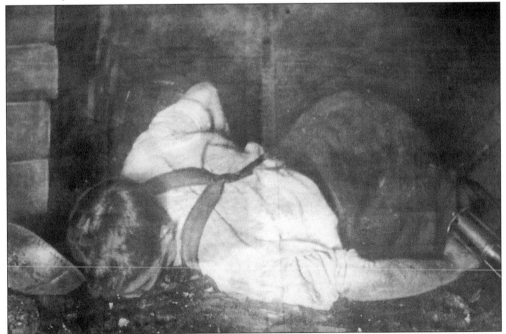

The explosion had gone full course killing 18 in the Tilley Seam, 63 in the Towneley Seam, 38 in the Busty Seam and 48 in the Brockwell Seam. Mark Henderson started to lead 34 men to safety but seven bolted for the shaft bottom and died. The 27 remaining miners began singing the hymn *Lead Kindly Light*. During the hymn young Jimmy Gardner, aged 14, died.

Henderson realised they would have to attempt to get out. Heading towards the shaft bottom he collapsed twice, falling over coal, timber and dead bodies. It was a quarter of a mile to the shaft bottom where he phoned the surface and informed them there were 26 alive. Henderson then made five more journeys back and forth bringing his men out in small groups.

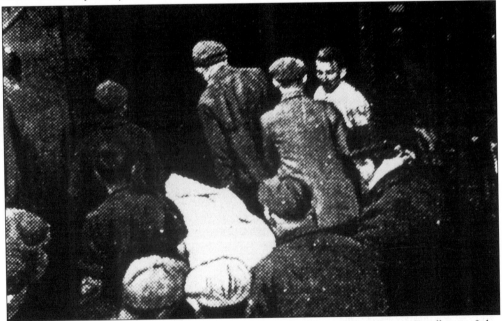

The last man rescued. Matt Elliott was rescued from the Busty Seam. Cogan Leadbitter, John Smith and last man out Paddy Joyce were rescued from the Towneley Seam. Joyce said that he and six others tried to escape the gas but one by one they had collapsed and died. He had luckily collapsed on loose coal where a trickle of fresh air came from below which saved his life.

Temporary coffins were made at the joiner shops for the unidentified bodies. The miners who died of gas were unmarked while others were difficult to recognise. A makeshift mortuary and hospital was set up in one of the buildings.

These men had a terrible task. They were posted as guards to keep away the rats. The injured miners lay separated from the dead by only a canvas and the living were affected by gasses from the bodies of the dead.

The dead miners were transported home by their loved ones on hand carts amidst huge crowds of onlookers.

The police estimated a crowd of around 20,000 would attend the funerals. In fact, on the first day, 200,000 filled the town to bursting point. Some families hired horse drawn hearses while poorer families had to have the coffins carried on the shoulders of friends and relatives.

The funerals come to a halt. Some of the coffins carried by relatives are seen here outside the Royal Hotel. The crowds engulfed them and several bearers collapsed. The Red Cross were on hand with smelling salts as grief was shared by the mass crowds.

STANLEY DISASTER
FUNERAL OF THE VICTIMS. FEB.21ˢᵗ 1909. (C)

The pit banner at the Stanley Inn. The funerals were headed by banners from the Durham Miners Association and the West Stanley Colliery (Burns). There was some effort to obtain crowd control but the situation was impossible.

STANLEY DISASTER
FUNERAL OF THE VICTIMS. FEB. 21ST 1909. (I)

It was at this point that everything came to a grinding halt. High Street, Front Street and Station Road were impassable in all directions. There was great distress for the relatives, unable to get their loved ones to the churchyard.

Stanley Pit Explosion, Feb 16th 1909.

Crowds at St Andrew's. Even at the church the situation was no better. St Andrew's was the public graveyard where members of all faiths, except the Roman Catholics, were buried. Services continued all day with several widows, overcome by grief, falling into the mass grave.

The mass graves were in the form of long trenches. In the distance are Simpson Street, Kay Street and Ridley Street. The Durham Light Infantry attended the last funeral on that first day at 5.30 pm. They fired a volley of shots over the grave and played the *Last Post* and the sound of the bugles filtered down into the valley below.

All the miners from the colliery were members of the Northumberland and Durham Permanent Relief Fund which meant the widows would receive 5 shillings per week and 2 shillings for each dependent child. A disaster fund raised £17,919 for the 238 dependants.

Workmen dig the mass grave in St Joseph's burial ground. The burial scenes here mirrored those seen at St Andrew's.

A lone boy stands viewing the flowers around the graves after the funerals. Iron railings were later erected around the site but sadly, these were removed for the war effort in the Second World War.

Kevin Keegan at the Memorial Service, 16 February 1995. Kevin's grandfather, Frank Keegan was one of those saved in 1909. After he was rescued, he went home, changed his clothes and returned to help other trapped miners. Kevin brought a team from Newcastle United to play a local side which helped raise funds for the building of the memorial which he unveiled at the Kings Head field.

Former miner, Michael Bailey started the fund for a permanent memorial, aided by Michael Brough, Derek Little and Joe Tyers. With the help of South Moor Police and Kevin Keegan, he raised £12,000. Michael is pictured through the pit wheel at the memorial service. It was his belief and driving force that made it all possible.

THE TRAGEDY OF THE MINE

The sixteenth of February, Nineteen Hundred and Nine,
Was a dreadful day, at West Stanley Mine,
That afternoon, at quarter to four,
A hundred and sixty eight lives, were to be no more,
A thunderous roar, through the town rang,
Fifty seconds later, came the big bang,
Everyone in Stanley, just froze for a bit,
They knew there was trouble at Burns pit,
Eye witnesses who had been standing close by,
Said the flames from the shaft had lit up the sky,
The whole town made their way to the pit head,
Not knowing then how many were dead,
As darkness fell the frost glistened bright,
They knew this would be a very long night,
Someone in the crowd said *Isn't it strange,*
It's the anniversary of the explosion at Trimdon Grange.
A small girl sobbed while saying a prayer,
Please Lord help me, my dad's down there,
Also down there, are my two brothers,
And its only a year since the death of my mother.
After eight hours waiting came a wonderful thing,
The Tilley seam telephone started to ring,
Mark Henderson called *There's twenty six of us here,*
That news made the crowd give a tremendous cheer.
Henderson's bravery, meant these men were alive,
He'd led them to safety in groups of five,
The rescuers toiled underground,
Till no more survivors could be found.
To have no father was many childrens fate,
Tommy Riley had eleven bairns, Luke Reay had eight,
The boy McGarry's body was found,
He'd gone down with his dad, to have *look around.*
Why he'd been down there, made people wonder,
He wasn't due to start work, till the following Monday,
The search was abandoned, for Rodgers and Chaytor,
Their remains were found, twenty four years later.
To remember these miners as each year goes,
Just think of a pack of dominoes,
Using this method, they won't be forgot,
Each victims represented by a spot.
Those men and boys, endured great pain,
Yet the loss of their lives had not been in vain,
The town was denuded of a generation,
But it forced the coal owners into new legislation.
In some homes in Stanley every Tuesday,
Is still referred to as bad news day,
Those miners went to work full of mirth,
And were all destroyed in the bowels of the earth.

by Michael Bailey

Eight

Sport

Burnhope Scratch cricket team. Regular team competitions were organised between scratch teams in the village. Great interest was shown in these matches and many a successful sportsman got his start after playing in such games.

East Stanley cricket team, *c*. 1930. Included in the team are; Ellis Wood, J. Williams, J. Nelson, W. Hair, R. Palmer, J. Uren, M. Wilson, J. Davenport, C. Shield, G. Carr, R. Temple, J. Dobson, J. Storey, J. Shield and D. Davison. The team played at the Welfare Ground which was levelled for use by local families around 1920.

The Board School swimming team, *c*. 1920. The school on Front Street had great success in local swimming competitions and the Blackett family had four sons in this team.

Craghead Welfare football team at the Old Craghead field adjacent to the aged miners' cottages in the 1940s. Included in the team are; mascot T. Bailey, H. Gregory, T. Gray, ? Welch, T. Greener, M. Heaviside, J. Pope, Piper Wilson, F. Weatherley, K. Welch, F. Elliott and trainer F. Bailey.

Shield Row School, 1938-39. This team were the Shimeld Bowl winners and included; J. Drummond (teacher), H. Barker, M. Gowland, Tot Laws, N. Keenan, E. Finlaw, L. Dowson, Titchy Steele and J. Kirkwood. The others are not known. Shield Row School opened 26 September 1932.

St Cuthbert's football team. The small mission church at East Stanley was well known for excellent sports teams.

Freddie Hall, Sunderland AFC, 1946/55. Fred was a no-nonsense, accomplished centre half. He was born at No Place and played much of his early football at East Stanley. His great love was pigeons and he had an excellent loft behind his Kip Hill home.

South Moor Tradesmen. This team played in the Wednesday league and were a match for most other sides. Included in the photograph are three members of the McPhail family; Hughie snr, Hughie jnr and Bob, who were local gents' hairdressers.

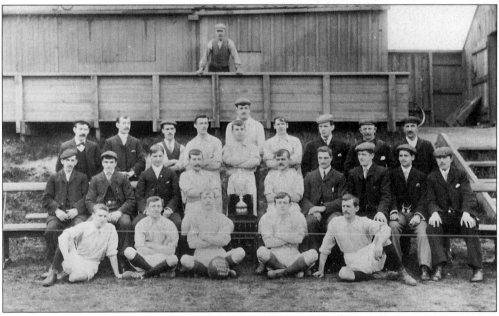

South Moor Violets, at the pavilion of South Moor cricket club, 1906. The man in the background is believed to be Robert Percival. He held the world cricket ball throwing record in 1882. A competition was held at Durham and he threw a cricket ball 140 yards 2 feet.

Billiard champions, at the entrance to Stanley Victoria Billiards Hall, *c.* 1947. The team are the winners of the Durham Miners Union Championship and include; Colin Simpson, Bob Waggott, Taffy Welch and ? Clarke.

Shield Row Athletic, *c.* 1950. The team are shown at an away cup competition and include; Pop Harrison, Billy Smith, Joe Wheelands, Charlie Sutherland, Jack Lister, Ron Dove, Bob Harrison jnr, Syd Wire, Jack Hawey, Jack Forster, Roy Hadrick, Ian Gibson, Jack Slater, Henry Clarke, Joe Rainbow and Tot Wallace.

Jack Hall of Quaking Houses
playing quoits at the 9th
Morrison Busty Welfare Schemes
Annual Childrens Sports Day
and Picnic at the Colliery
Welfare field, 1964.

Stanley Victoria at Oakey's field, 1947. This team and others played games to raise funds for the
Morrison/Louisa disaster fund. The team includes; J. Robson, P. English, G. Fishburn, T. Elliott,
T. Urwin, W. Woods, J. Lidster, J. Robson, W. Robinson, J. Johnson, T. Benfield, W. Diss,
J. Harrison, S. Clarke, E. Fishburn, J. Elliott and F. Cousins.

Glen McCrory and Mary Armstrong. Annfield Plain born Glen is the former cruiserweight champion of the world. He is shown here with the championship belt he won after beating Pat Lumumba at Stanley Sports Centre. Mary is also a 'champion' after becoming the first woman chairperson of Derwentside District Council.

Towneley sports day, 1965. The athletics team includes; Tom Salkeld, excellent at track, field, cross country and football, Joe Young, a cross country runner, Alan Harrison, sprinter, PE teacher Pat McCue and John Hughes, who was excellent with the javelin.

A group of Stanley boxers, *c.* 1933. Back row: left to right, Tommy Broughy (trainer), Joe Broughy, Teddy Joyce, Barney Whitney (manager). Seated: Miley Connolly and Bud Rogers. These fighters and other greats including George Harwood, Ted Barrass and Tom Pinkney were legends in local boxing circles in the 1920s and '30s.

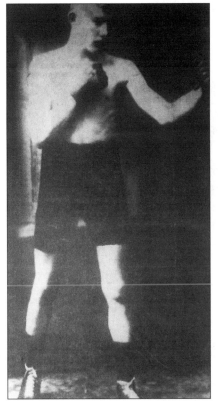

Joe Broughy was born in 1913, the 11th of 12 children. He became Pitmen's lightweight champion in 1933 at West Stanley football ground when he out-pointed the holder Mattie Hinds of Belmont. Tragically Joe became a victim of Leukaemia and died in 1956, aged 43.

Miley Connolly was born at Quaking Houses in 1914. His career began in the 1930s as a southpaw welterweight. He had a no-nonsense style of punching which made him very popular. He resumed his boxing career after the Second World War winning three fights between 1945-47.

Joe Broughly, Miley Connolly and Hughie McPhail. Broughy became a professional in 1932. His career was cut short by an injury in the pits. Connolly became a professional in 1931. He had over 100 official contests although he fought many more in the fairground boxing booths.

Teddy Joyce was a rugged middleweight scrapper. Joyce fought during the Broughy-Connolly era before moving to Coventry in the 1950s.

Ken McMahon, born in 1932, began his boxing career at Stanley Boys Club aged 14. His trainers were Edward G. Robinson and Harry Scott. He trained three times a week at the club and sparred with older brother John. Ken had 64 fights, from bantamweight to light-welterweight and lost only four contests.

Ken and John McMahon. Ken, on the left, won the Northern Counties Boys Club championship at 15. He also won the Northern Counties Junior ABA and the N.C.B. Northern Counties Junior championship. At 18 he won the Durham Coal Board championship. John began his career at lightweight before moving to welterweight.

Len Simpson began his boxing career at Stanley Boys Club which was run by the retired boxer Edward G. Robinson. Here he met and trained with other local boxers such as Leo and Ted Hodgon, and Ken and John McMahon. Len's greatest triumph was winning the N.C.B. light-heavyweight championship in 1964.